# ATLAS
## OF ELEMENTARY
# BOTANY

Copyright © 2025 by Schiffer Publishing, Ltd.

Originally published as *Atlas de Botanique Élémentaire* by Flammarion, Paris © 2021
Translated from the French by Rebecca DeWald

Library of Congress Control Number: 2024946207

All rights reserved. No part of this work may be reproduced or used in any form or by any means—graphic, electronic, or mechanical, including photocopying or information storage and retrieval systems—without written permission from the publisher.

The scanning, uploading, and distribution of this book or any part thereof via the Internet or any other means without the permission of the publisher is illegal and punishable by law. Please purchase only authorized editions and do not participate in or encourage the electronic piracy of copyrighted materials.

"Schiffer," "Schiffer Publishing, Ltd.," and the pen and inkwell logo are registered trademarks of Schiffer Publishing, Ltd.

Type set in DTLParadoxST/Neutraface 2 Display/Brandon Grotesque

ISBN: 978-0-7643-6952-0
Printed in China

Published by Schiffer Publishing, Ltd.
4880 Lower Valley Road
Atglen, PA 19310
Phone: (610) 593-1777; Fax: (610) 593-2002
Email: Info@schifferbooks.com
Web: www.schifferbooks.com

For our complete selection of fine books on this and related subjects, please visit our website at www.schifferbooks.com. You may also write for a free catalog.

Schiffer Publishing's titles are available at special discounts for bulk purchases for sales promotions or premiums. Special editions, including personalized covers, corporate imprints, and excerpts, can be created in large quantities for special needs. For more information, contact the publisher.

We are always looking for people to write books on new and related subjects. If you have an idea for a book, please contact us at proposals@schifferbooks.com.

**JEAN-JACQUES ROUSSEAU**

ILLUSTRATIONS BY KARIN DOERING-FROGER

# ATLAS
## OF ELEMENTARY
# BOTANY

PREFACE BY MARC JEANSON

4880 Lower Valley Road • Atglen, PA 19310

# PREFACE

*The study of nature detaches us from ourselves and elevates us to its author. It is in this sense that one truly becomes a philosopher; it is in this way that natural history and botany have a use for wisdom and for virtue.*
—Letter to the Duchess of Portland, September 3, 1766
(trans. by Philip Stewart and Jean Vaché)

This quote is perhaps exemplary of the way in which Rousseau establishes the most beautiful exchange, which would become so dear to him, between the disciplines of descriptive botany and philosophy. Even though the definition of philosophy has nowadays evolved—as have botanical concepts accepted in the eighteenth century—it is worth noting that Rousseau assigned to botany a more fundamental role than many of his contemporaries did, for whom this "lovely science" was a respectable discipline but of relatively minor impact.

The eight letters that make up this collection were written between August 22, 1771, and April 11, 1774. They were intended for a close friend of Rousseau's, Madeleine Catherine Delessert, whom he affectionately called "dear cousin" and who wanted to teach botany to her daughter Madelon. To this series of letters, Rousseau added a "pedagogical" herbarium, which allowed his young pupil and her mother to observe the morphological details described in the letters with their own eyes. The eighth and last letter thus discusses herbaria and how to assemble them.

In the second Dialogue of his *Rousseau, Judge of Jean-Jacques*, he returns to the conditions under which this modest hortus siccus of 167 sheets was created:

"By extensive and frequent herborizing, he made an immense collection of plants. He dried them with infinite care, glued them with great neatness onto paper which he decorated with red frames. He was careful to preserve the aspect and color of the flowers and the leaves, to the extent of making these herb books prepared in this way into collections of miniatures" (trans. by Roger D. Masters and Christopher Kelly).

It may be that Rousseau thus triggered an interest in botany that would captivate generation upon generation of the Delessert family and eventually culminated in the all-encompassing endeavor of Benjamin Delessert: the father of the industrial extraction of sugar from sugar beet, a nephew of Madelon's, would become the originator of one of the most beautiful botanical collections of the nineteenth century.

Rousseau's interest in botany stemmed from an accidental encounter on the side of a road in Les Charmettes, at the end of the summer of 1735. The person who, up until then, somewhat held the "botany of apothecaries" in contempt is suddenly seduced and fascinated by the blue blossom of a periwinkle that, unexpectedly and out of season, bloomed in a hedge. Although the vision of this bright flower would remain engraved in his memory forever, his entire work as a botanist would oppose a purely visual apprehension of flora, as he establishes in his first letter: "Besides, merely to be acquainted with plants by sight, and to know only their names, cannot but be too insipid a study for a genius like yours; and it may be presumed that your daughter would not be long amused with it" (trans. by Thomas Martyn). Rousseau is above all a describer of botany who likes to observe and name the structures and organs of plants.

It bears some significance that he owes this initial emotion to the humble periwinkle, triggering a first interest that is not purely aesthetic but is directed at the very nature of the plant. Over time, he would devote most of his time to flowers in particular. These letters are a perfect reflection of that.

In the mid-eighteenth century, the most-prominent plant classification systems were essentially based on the organs of flowers and their organization. Tournefort's system classified flowering plants according to the presence or absence of the corolla and the structure of the latter, while radically rejecting the notion of sexual differentiation in plants foregrounded by Rudolph Jacob Camerarius in 1694. Carl von Linné (Linnaeus) drew inspiration from Camerarius's work to establish his plant classification system called the "sexual system," in which he organized flowering plants according to the number and arrangement of their sexual organs: pistils and stamens were the only organs on which botanists must focus their attention to establish the group of plants to which the species under observation belongs.

These so-called "artificial" classification systems—because they take into account only the organs of flowers and ignore other vegetative characteristics (leaves, veins, etc.)—would eventually be replaced by so-called "natural" systems, put forward in Paris by Michel Adanson or Bernard and Antoine Laurent de Jussieu, among others. Rousseau would remain faithful to the sexual system developed by Linné throughout his life.

More than a mere series of lessons for the young Mademoiselle Delessert, reading these educational letters seems like a real invitation for us to observe, and to dive right into the world of flowers. But not just any flowers, since Rousseau undoubtedly specifies the focus of his attention: he is interested, he tells us, only in wildflowers and, sticking to his convictions, advises being wary of so-called horticultural plants, which are, in his eyes, truly disfigured monsters selected and multiplied by humankind.

The origin of plants is another point on which Rousseau's opinion would radically change over time, and quickly so. Throughout his life, he had expressed nothing but contempt for plants he called "foreign"—we would call them nonnative today—since he preferred by far the hay he found under his feet. This very "indigenist" vision of flora would disappear at the very end of his life. The late and nonetheless intense rekindling of his passion for botany, which struck him shortly before his death, moved him to embark on a wild herbarium project with the aim of assembling all the plants of the earth. It was for this purpose that he acquired a collection, which is to this day kept at the Herbarium of the Muséum National d'Histoire Naturelle in Paris. The collection consists of fifteen cardboard binders containing 494 specimens organized according to the Linnaean classification system. The aesthetic characteristic of Rousseau's specimens is that the dried plants are presented framed with three lines of red ink. A considerable proportion of the plants in this collection were originally brought together by the botanist Jean Baptiste Christophore Fusée-Aublet, who was very active in French Guiana. The shapes and features of these plants are therefore typical of tropical (i.e., nonnative) plants.

For Rousseau, following the zeitgeist of his century, when the hollowing out of biodiversity did not yet make headline news, botany was "a study of pure curiosity and has no other real use than that, which a thinking sensible being may deduce from the observation of nature and the wonders of the universe" (trans. Thomas Martyn). In his opinion, we "must not . . . give more importance to botany than it really has" (ibid.). Public perception is certainly radically different from that in the early twenty-first century.

# PREFACE

Among the dried specimens that Rousseau consulted in the last months of his life, and that are now kept in the herbarium at the Muséum, there are nomenclatural items.

These are reference specimens, yardsticks against which to measure each species name, which is essential to correctly name plants. On these dried plants, affixed with a fragile strip of paper, rests the reliability of any study of plants. Genetics, phytochemistry, pharmaceutics: no scientific study can be conducted without the ability to reliably name the organism under scrutiny.

The information associated with each of these specimens (location and date of collection) also forms a unique and indispensable reference frame to accurately document, over the centuries, the changes affecting the flora of the world and the evolution of various threatened or invasive species populations.

Just like Rousseau, many citizens and decision makers of today consider botany to be merely a lovely science, a pastime for geeky oldies, though it has never been more crucial to observe plants and to describe, name, and collect them in the form of herbaria and seed banks.

The acceleration and constant rise of the movement of people have led to a large-scale cross-fertilization of species, which impacts various changes worldwide and fuels the ever-increasing human footprint: we are in a time of digits, decimal degrees, and the number of endangered species. Environmentalism, like worries, has become a global concern.

However, nothing can be preserved without being identified first. Forests are destroyed or are changing face, but to be able to quantify the scale of destruction, we must name the species that make up the woods. Isn't the intention of an ecological restoration project intimately linked to the species employed?

How can we pursue the great inventory of the living world we have barely even begun without observation and description? How to characterize and halt the disappearance of biodiversity without identifying living species?

Environmentalism and environmentalists remind us of alarming trends, thousands of endangered species, percentages, and the sixth mass extinction. This is essential and indisputable. The Greta Thunberg generation is discovering the living world through the prism of an avalanche of figures and projections. But do they get to observe plants? Do they know that involucre and pappus, corolla and stipule, are key components of this fight?

That is why I am delighted that these botanical letters are being reissued. At a time when fundamental questions, fear, and disturbing trends occupy every space and consume the living world, let us reconnect with slow wanderings, herbaria, and patient observation, the sources of wonder and discovery of tiny worlds of infinite beauty.

Let us put hay in our heads.

Marc Jeanson

*« I love botany:*
*It is getting worse every day,*
*I have only hay in my head.*
*One of these mornings I will turn into a plant.*
*(anonymous translation) »*

# LETTERS ON THE ELEMENTS OF BOTANY, ADDRESSED TO A LADY

# LETTER I

On the Fructification and Liliaceous Plants • August, 22, 1771

I think your idea of amusing the vivacity of your daughter a little, and exercising her attention upon such agreeable and varied objects as plants, is excellent: though I should not have ventured to play the pedant so far as to propose it of myself. Since, however, it comes from you, I approve it with all my heart and will even assist you in it. Convinced that, at all times of life, the study of nature abates the taste for frivolous amusements, prevents the tumult of the passions, and provides the mind with a nourishment that is salutary, by filling it with an object most worthy of its contemplations.

You have begun with teaching your daughter the names of the common plants that you have about you; this was the very thing you should have done. The few plants that she knows by sight are so many points of comparison for her to extend her knowledge: but they are not sufficient. You desire to have a little catalog of the most-common plants, with the marks by which they may be known. I find some difficulty in doing this for you: that is, in giving you these marks or characters in writing, after a manner that is clear, and at the same time not diffuse. This seems impossible without using the language peculiar to the subject, and the terms of that language form a vocabulary apart, which you cannot understand unless it be previously explained to you.

Besides, merely to be acquainted with plants by sight, and to know only their names, cannot but be too insipid a study for a genius like yours, and it may be presumed that your daughter would not be long amused with it. I propose that you should have some preliminary notions of the vegetable structure or organization of plants, in order that you may get some real information, though you were to take only a few steps into the most beautiful and the richest of the three kingdoms of nature. We have nothing therefore to do yet with the nomenclature, which is but the knowledge of a herbalist.

I have always thought it possible to be a very great botanist without knowing so much as one plant by name, and, without wishing to make your daughter a very great botanist, I think nevertheless that it will always be useful to her to learn how to see, whatever she looks at, well. Do not, however, be terrified at the undertaking: you will soon know that it is not a great one. There is nothing either complicated or difficult in what I have to propose to you. Nothing is required but to have patience to begin with the beginning. After that, you may go on no further than you choose.

We are now getting toward the latter season, and those plants that are the most simple in their structure are already past. Besides, I expect you will take some time to make your observations a little regularly. However, in the meanwhile, until spring puts you in a situation to begin and follow the order of nature, I am going to give you a few words of the vocabulary to get by heart.

A perfect plant is composed of a root, of a stem with its branches, of leaves, flower, and fruit (for in botany, by fruit, in herbs as well as in trees, we understand the whole fabric of the seed). You know the whole of this already, at least enough to understand the term, but there is a principal part that requires an examination more at large; I mean the fructification, that is, the flower and the fruit. Let us begin with the flower, which comes first.

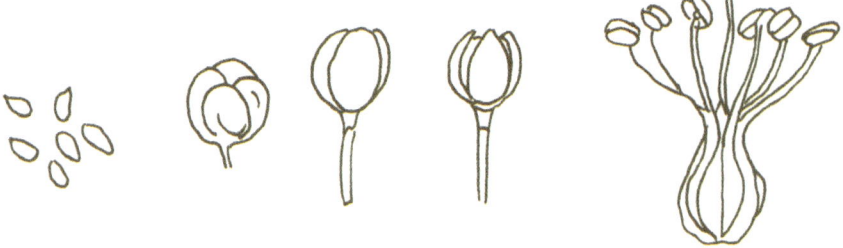

In this part, nature has enclosed the summary of her work; by this she perpetuates it, and this also is commonly the most brilliant of all parts of the vegetable, and always least liable to variations.

Take a lily: I believe you will easily find it still in full flower. Before it opens, you see at the top of the stem an oblong greenish bud, which grows whiter the nearer it is to opening, and when it is quite open, you perceive that the white cover takes the form of a basin or vase divided into several segments. This is called the corol, and not the flower, as it is by the vulgar, because the flower is a composition of several parts, of which the corol is only the principal.

The corol of the lily is not of one piece, as you easily see. When it withers and falls, it separates into six distinct pieces, which are called petals. Thus the corol of the lily is composed of six petals. A corol consisting of several pieces like this is called a polypetalous corol. If it were all of one piece, like the bellflower, or bindweeds, it would be called monopetalous. But to return to our lily.

You will find exactly in the middle of the corol a sort of little column rising from the bottom and pointing directly upward. This, taken in its whole, is called the pistil or pointal: taken in its parts, it is divided into three: (1) the swollen base, with three blunted angles, called the germ or ovary; (2) a thread placed upon this, called the style; (3) the style crowned by a sort of capital with three notches: this capital is called the stigma. Here you have the components of the pistil and its three constituent parts.

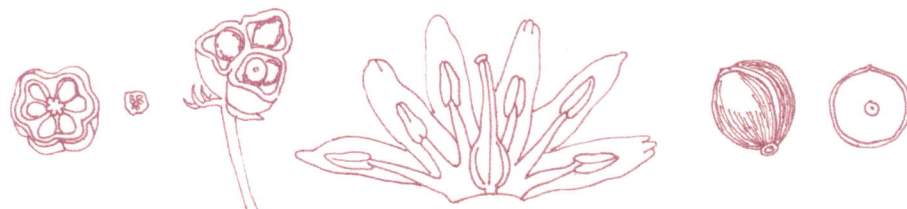

Between the pistil and the corol you find six other bodies entirely separate from each other, which are called the stamens. Each stamen is composed of two parts, one long and thin, by which it is fastened to the bottom of the corol, and called the filament; the other thicker, placed at the top of the filament, and called anther. Each anther is a box that opens when it is ripe, and throws out a yellow dust, which has a strong smell: this is called pollen or farina.

Such is the general analysis of the parts that constitute a flower. As the corol fades and falls, the germ increases and becomes an oblong triangular capsule, within which are flat seeds in three cells. This capsule, considered as the cover of the seeds, takes the name of pericarp. But I will not undertake an analysis of the fruit here: this will form the subject of another letter.

The parts here mentioned are found in the flowers of most other plants, but in different proportion, situation, and number.

By the analogy of these parts, and their different combinations, the families of the vegetable kingdom are determined: and these analogies are connected with others in those parts of the plant that seem to have no relation to them. For instance, this number of six stamens, sometimes only

three, of six petals or divisions of the corol, and that triangular form of the germ, with its three cells, determine the liliaceous tribe, and in all this tribe, which is very numerous, the roots are bulbs of some sort or other. That of the lily is (squamous, or) composed of scales; in the asphodel, it is a number of oblong solid bulbs connected together; in the (crocus and) saffron there are two bulbs, one over the other; in the colchicum they are placed side by side.

The lily, which I have chosen because it is in season, and also on account of the size of the flower and its other parts, is deficient, however, in one of the constituent parts of a perfect flower; namely, the calyx, which is that outer green part of the flower usually divided into five parts or composed of five small leaves, sustaining and embracing the corol at the bottom and enveloping it entirely before it opens, as you may have remarked in the rose.

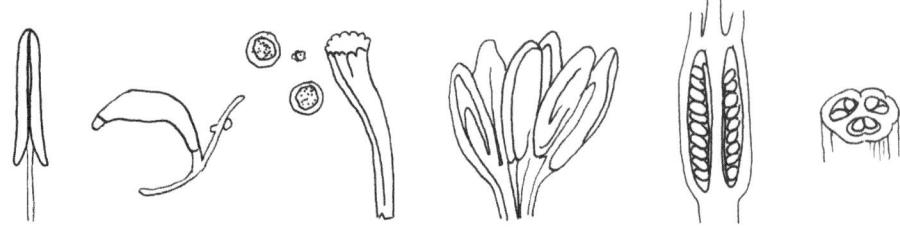

The calyx, which accompanies almost all other flowers, is wanting in the greater part of the liliaceous tribe; as the tulip, the hyacinth, the narcissus, the tuberose, etc. and even in the onion, leek, garlic, etc., which are also liliaceous, though they appear very different at first sight. You will perceive also that in this whole tribe the stems are simple and unbranched, the leaves entire and never cut or divided, observations that confirm the analogy of the flower and fruit in this family, by that of the other parts of the plants. If you bestow some attention upon these particulars and make them familiar to you by frequent observations, you are already in a condition to determine, by an attentive and continued inspection of a plant, whether it be of the liliaceous tribe or not, and this without knowing the name of the plant. You see that this is not a mere labor of the memory, but a study of observations and facts truly worthy of a naturalist. You will not begin by telling your daughter all this at once, and still less when in the sequel you shall be initiated in the mysteries of vegetation, but you will unveil to her by degrees no more than is suitable to her age and sex, by directing her how to find out things of herself, rather than by teaching her. Adieu, my dear cousin; if all this trash be agreeable to you, I am at your service.

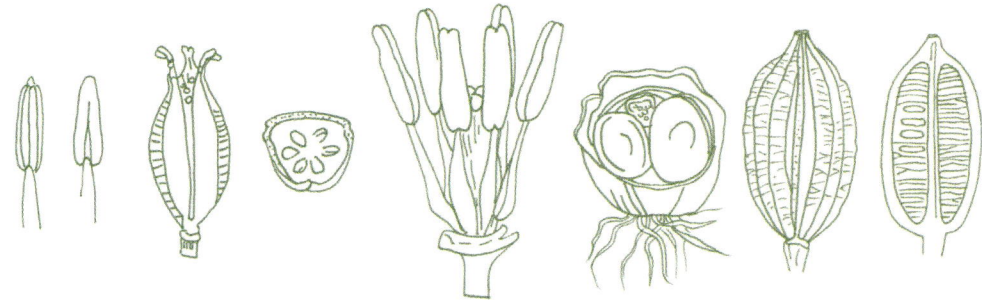

# LETTER II

On Cruciform Flowers • October 18, 1771

Since you understand so well, my dear cousin, the first lineaments of plants, though so slightly marked, as to be able already to distinguish the liliaceous family by their air, and since our little botanist amuses herself with corols and petals, I am going to set before you another tribe, upon which she may again exercise her little knowledge; with rather more difficulty, I own, because the flowers are much smaller and the foliage more varied, but with the same pleasure both on her side and on yours; at least if you have as much delight in following this flowery path as I find in tracing it out to you.

When the first rays of spring shall have enlightened your progress, by shewing you in the gardens hyacinths, tulips, narcissuses, jonquils, and lilies of the valley, the analysis of all which is already known to you, other flowers will soon catch your attention and require of you a new examination; such are wallflowers and stocks gilliflowers and dame's rockets. Whenever you find them double, do not meddle with them; they are disfigured or, if you please, dressed after our fashion: nature will no longer be found among them; she refuses to reproduce any thing from monsters thus mutilated: for if the most brilliant part of the flower, namely the corol, is multiplied, it is at the expense of the more essential parts, which disappear under this addition of brilliancy.

Take then a single stock gilliflower (or stock, as it is vulgarly called) and proceed to the analysis of the flower: you will perceive immediately an exterior part, which was wanting in the liliaceous flowers; namely, the calyx. This consists of four pieces, which we must call leaves, leaflets, or folioles, having no proper names to express them by, as we have that of petals for the pieces that compose the corol. These four pieces are commonly unequal by pairs; that is, there are

## ATLAS OF ELEMENTARY BOTANY

two leaflets opposite and equal, of a smaller size, and two others also opposite and equal, but larger, especially toward the bottom, where they are so rounded as to exhibit a very sensible protuberance or bump on the outside.

In this calyx you will find a corol composed of four petals. I say nothing of their color, because that makes no part of their character. Each of these petals is fastened to the receptacle, or bottom of the calyx, by a narrow pale part, which is called unguis (or the tail of the petal), and this spreads out over the top of the calyx into a large, flat, colored part, called lamina (or the border).

In the center of the corol is one pistil, long and cylindric, or nearly so, chiefly composed of a germ ending in a very short style, and that terminated by an oblong stigma, which is bifid, that is to say, divided into two parts, which are reflected on each side.

If you examine carefully the respective position of the calyx and corol, you will see that each petal, instead of corresponding exactly to each leaflet of the calyx, is, on the contrary, placed between two, so that it answers to the opening that separates them, and this alternate position has place in all flowers that have as many petals to the corol as leaflets to the calyx.

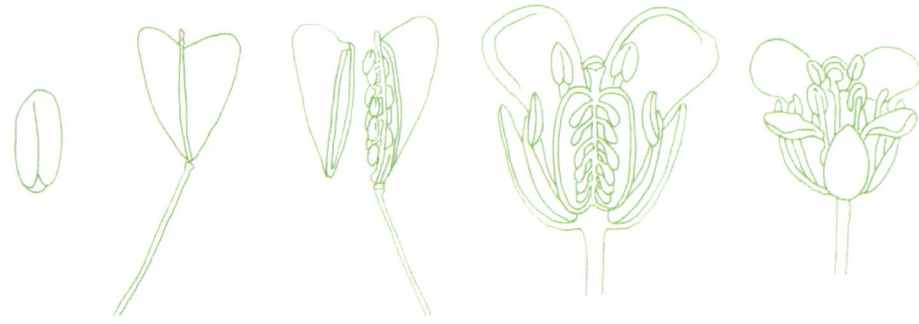

It remains now to speak of the stamens. You will find six of them in the flower of the stock, as in the liliaceous flowers, but not all equal, or else alternately unequal, as in those, but you will perceive two opposite to each other, sensibly shorter than the other four that separate them, and that are also separate from each other in pairs.

I shall not enter here into a detail of their structure and position: but I give you notice that if you look carefully you will find the reason why these two stamens are shorter than the other four, and why two leaflets of the calyx are more protuberant, or, as the botanists speak, more gibbous, and the other two more flatted.

To finish the history of our stock, you must not abandon it as soon as you have analyzed the flower, but wait until the corol withers and falls, which it does pretty soon, and then remark what becomes of the pistil, composed, as we observed before, of the germ, the style, and the stigma. The germ grows considerably in length and thickens a little as the fruit ripens. When it is ripe, it becomes a kind of flat pod, called silique.

This silique is composed of two valves, each covering a small cell: and the cells are separated by a thin partition.

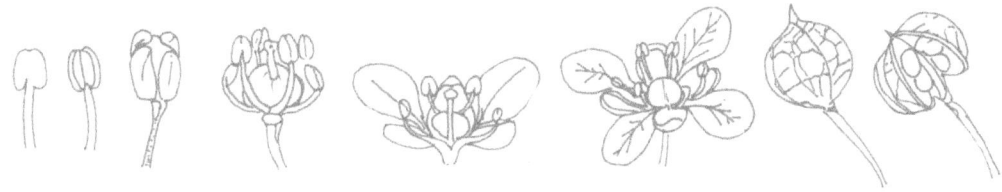

When the seed is ripe, the valves open from the bottom upward to give it passage and remain fast to the stigma at top. Then you may see that flat, round seeds ranged along each side of the partition, and you will find that they are fastened alternately to right and left by a short pedicle to the sutures, or each edge of the partition, by which the sides are as if sewed together with the valves before their separation occurred.

I am very much afraid, my dear cousin, that I have fatigued you a little with this long description, but it was necessary to give you the essential character of the numerous tribe of cruciform flowers, which forms an entire class in almost all the systems of botanists: and I hope that this description, which it is difficult to understand here without a figure, will become more intelligible when you shall have gone through it with some attention, having at the same time the object before your eyes.

The great number of species in this class has determined botanists to divide it into two sections, in which the flowers are perfectly alike, but the fruits (pericarps, or seed vessels) are sensibly different.

The first order comprehends the cruciform flowers with a silique, or pod, such as the stock, those mentioned in note (m), and the like.

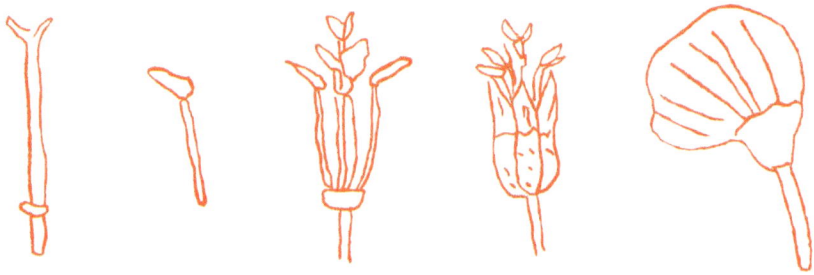

The second contains those whose seed vessel is a silicle; that is, a small and very short pod, almost as wide as it is long, and differently divided within, as whitlow grass, mithridate mustard, bastard cress, etc. in the fields and scurvy grass, horseradish, candy tuft, honesty, etc. in the gardens: though the seed vessel of the last is very large, it is still a silicle, because the length exceeds the breadth very little. If none of these are known to you, I presume at least that you are acquainted with the shepherd's purse, which is so common a weed in kitchen gardens. Well, then, cousin, this shepherd's purse is of the cruciform tribe, and the silicle branch of it, and the form of the silicle is triangular. By this you may form some idea of the rest until they fall into your hands.

But it is time to let you breathe, hoping that this letter, when the season allows you to make good use of it, will be followed by many more, in which I shall have the chance to elaborate on what there remains to say about the cruciform tribe, and which I have neglected to say here; I will only therefore give you a hint at present that in this class, and many others, you will often find flowers much smaller than those of the stock, and sometimes so small that you cannot examine their parts without the assistance of a glass, an instrument that a

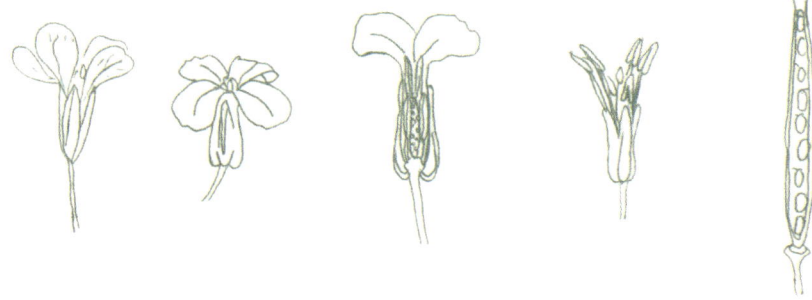

botanist cannot do without any more than he can without a needle, a lancet, or penknife, and a pair of good scissors. Presuming that your maternal zeal may carry you thus far, I fancy to myself a charming picture of my beautiful cousin busy with her glass examining heaps of flowers, a hundred times less flourishing, less fresh, and less agreeable than herself. Adieu, dear cousin, until the next chapter.

# LETTER III

Of Papilionaceous Flowers • May 26, 1772

I suppose, dear cousin, that my previous response has reached you well, although you do not make mention of it in your second letter. In this response to it here, I hope, concluding from your account, that Mother has recovered well and has left for Switzerland in good spirits. Since Aunt Julie ought to have left with her, I have entrusted M.G., who will return to Val-de-Travers with the little herbarium for her and will have it delivered to your address, so that you may, in her absence, receive and use it, should you encounter something useful for your purposes in this crude collection of specimen. Beyond that, I do not think you have any claim to this heap of papers. You do, however, have a claim to the person who assembled it, and the strongest and dearest I can think of, but the hortus siccus was promised to your sister when she collected plants with me on our promenades at the crossroads of Vague, so you must not consider anything less than those walks when my heart and my feet were following you with Grandmother in Vaise. I blush at the thought of having spoken to her so late and so poorly; in this regard, she has received word from me and precedence over you. As regards you, my dear cousin, even though I will not promise you a herbarium made by my hands, you will receive a more precious one made by the hands of your daughter if you continue to pursue with her that peaceable and delightful study that fills up those voids in our time that others dedicate to idleness, or something worse, with interesting observations on nature; I will resume the interrupted thread of our vegetable tribes.

My intention is to describe six of these tribes to you first, in order to render the general structure of the characteristic parts of plants familiar. You have already had two of them; there are four remaining, which you must still have the patience to go through, and after that, quitting for a time the other branches of that numerous race, and going on to examine the different parts of the fructification, we shall manage so, that without knowing many plants, perhaps, you will at least never be in a strange country among the productions of the vegetable kingdom.

But I must inform you that if you will take books in hand and pursue the common nomenclature, with abundance of names, you will have few ideas; those that you have will be confused, and you will not follow properly either my steps or those of others but will have at most a mere knowledge of words. I am jealous, dear cousin, of being your only guide in this part of botany. When it is the proper time I will point out to you the books that you may consult. In the meantime, have patience to read nothing but in that of nature, and to keep wholly to my letters.

Peas are, at present, in full fructification. Seize the moment to observe their characters: they are some of the most curious that botany affords. One general division of flowers is into regular and irregular. The first are they whose parts all spring uniformly from the center of the flower and terminate in the circumference of a circle. This uniformity is the reason why when we view flowers of this kind, we do not distinguish an under from an upper part, or the right from the left; such are the two tribes that we have already examined.

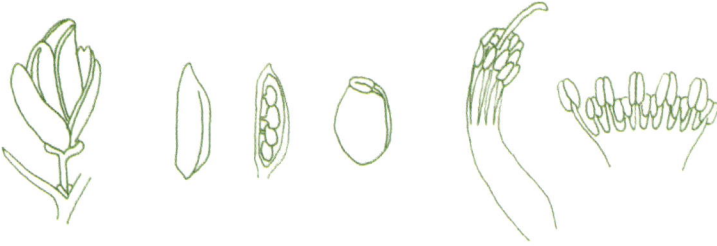

But you will see at first sight that the flower of the pea is irregular, that you easily distinguish the longer part of the corol, which should be at top, from the shorter, which should be at bottom, and you know very well, when you hold up the flower to the eye, whether it be in its natural situation or not. Thus in examining an irregular flower, whenever we speak of the top and the bottom, we suppose it to be in its natural situation.

The flowers of this tribe being of a very particular structure, you not only must have several pea flowers, and dissect them successively, to observe all their parts one after another, but you also must pursue the progress of the fructification from the first flowering to the maturity of the fruit.

First, you will find a monophyllous calyx; that is, one of an entire piece, ending in five very distinct points, the two wider of which are at top, and three narrower at bottom. This calyx bends toward the lower part, as does also the peduncle, or little stalk that supports it: this peduncle is very small and easily movable, so that the flower readily avoids a current of air and commonly turns its back to the wind and rain.

Having examined the calyx, you may pull it off, so as to leave the rest of the flower entire, and then you will see plainly that the corol is polypetalous.

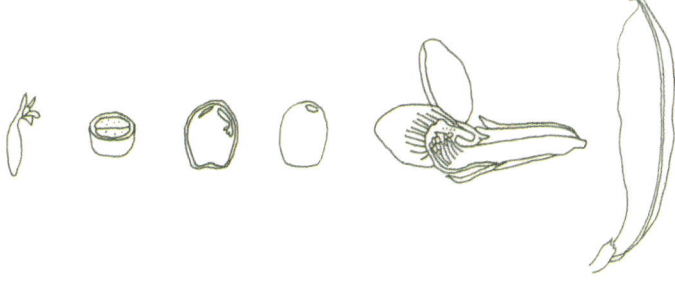

The first piece is a large white petal, covering the others and occupying the upper part of the corol; it is called standard, or banner. We must make use neither of our eyes nor of common sense, if we do not perceive that this petal is designed to protect the other parts of the flower from the principal injuries of the weather. In taking off the standard, you will observe that it is inserted on each side by a little process into the side pieces, so that it cannot be driven out of its place by the wind.

The standard being taken off exposes to view those two side pieces to which it adhered; they are called the wings. In taking these off, you will find them still more strongly inserted into the remaining part, so that they cannot be separated without some effort. These wings are scarcely less useful in protecting the sides of the flower than the standard in covering it.

Taking off the wings, you discover the last piece of the corol; this is that which covers and defends the center of the flower and wraps it up, especially underneath, as carefully as the three other petals envelop the upper part and the sides. This last piece, which on account of its form is called the boat or keel, is, as it were, the strongbox into which nature has put her treasure to keep it safe from the attacks of air and water.

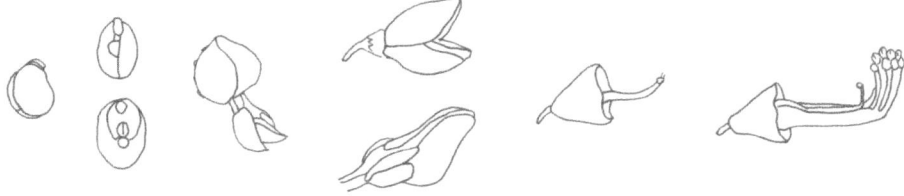

When you have well examined this petal, draw it gently downward, pinching it slightly by the keel or thin edge, for fear of tearing away what it contains. I am certain you will be pleased with the mystery it reveals when the veil is removed. The young fruit involved in the boat or keel is constructed in this manner: a cylindric membrane, terminated by ten distinct threads, surrounds the germ, or embryo, of the legume or pod. These ten threads are so many filaments, united below around the germ and each terminated by a yellow anther, whose farina covers the stigma, which terminates the style, or grows along the side of it: this stigma, though yellow with the meal that sticks to it, is easily distinguished by its figure and size. Thus do these ten filaments form also about the germ an interior armor, to preserve it from exterior injuries.

If you examine more curiously, you will find that these ten filaments are united into one at the base, only in appearance. For in the upper part of this cylinder, there is a piece or stamen that at first appears to adhere to the rest but, as the flower fades and the fruit increases, separates and leaves an opening at top, by which the fruit can extend itself by opening and separating the cylinder gradually, which otherwise, by compressing and straightening it all around, would impede its growth. If the flower is not sufficiently advanced, you will not find this stamen detached from the cylinder, but put a fine pin or needle into two little holes that you will see near the receptacle, at the base of that stamen, and you will soon perceive the stamen with its anther separate from the nine others, which will always continue to form one body, until at length they fade and dry when the germ becomes a legume and has no longer any occasion for them.

This legume, whose germ changes as it matures, is distinguished from the silique of the cruciform tribe by the seeds being fastened to one side only of the case, alternately indeed to each valve of it, but all of them to the same side. You will understand this distinction perfectly if you open the pod of a pea and of a stock at the same time, taking care only to have them before they are quite ripe, so that, when the pericarp is opened, the seeds may continue fastened by their proper ligaments to their sutures and their valves.

If I have made myself well understood, you will comprehend, dear cousin, what astonishing precautions have been heaped together by nature to bring the embryo of the pea to maturity, and, above all, to protect it in the midst of the greatest rains from that wet, which is fatal to it, without enclosing it in a hard shell, which would have made it another kind of fruit. The Creator, attentive to the preservation of all beings, has taken great care to protect the fructification of plants from attacks that may injure it, but he seems to have doubled his attention to those that serve for the nourishment of man and animals, as does the greater part of the leguminous or pulse tribe. The provision for the fructification of peas is, in different proportions, the same through this class. The flowers have the name of papilionaceous, from a fancied resemblance of them to the form of a butterfly (papilio); they generally have a standard or banner, two wings, and a boat or keel; that is, four irregular petals. But in some genera the boat is divided longitudinally into two pieces almost adhering by the keel, and these flowers have in reality five petals: others, such as clover, have all their petals united and, though papilionaceous, are however monopetalous flowers.

The papilionaceous or leguminous plants form one of the most numerous and useful tribes. Beans, peas, lucerne, saintfoin, clover, lupins, lentils, tares or vetches, indigo, liquorice, kidney beans, etc. all belong to it: the character of these last is to have the boat literally twisted, which at first might be taken for an accident. There are also some trees belonging to it, among others that which is commonly called acacia but is not the true acacia, and many beautiful flowering shrubs. But of these, more hereafter. Adieu, cousin; I wish well to everything that you love.

# LETTER IV

Of Labiate and Personate Flowers • June, 19, 1772

(Let us talk of plants, my dear cousin, while the season for observing them invites us.) Your solution of my question concerning the stamens of cruciform flowers is perfectly right and shows that you have understood me, or rather attended to me, for you have nothing to do but to attend in order to understand. You have accounted very well for the swellings of the two leaflets of the calyx, and the relative shortness of two of the stamens, in the stock, by the bending of these two stamens. One step more would have led you to the primary cause of this structure: for if you ask once more why these stamens are thus bent, and consequently shortened? I answer that you will find a little gland upon the receptacle, between the stamen and the germ, and it is this gland that, by throwing the stamen to a distance and forcing it to take a round, necessarily shortens it. Upon the same receptacle are two other glands, one at the foot of each pair of longer stamens, but being on the outside of them, between these stamens and the calyx, they do not oblige them to bend and therefore do not shorten them: so that the two pairs of stamens stand higher than the two single bent ones; not because they are longer, but because they are straight. These four glands, or at least vestiges of them, are more or less visible in almost all cruciform flowers and are much more distinct in some than in the stock. If you ask me what the glands are for, I answer that they are one of those instruments destined by nature to unite the vegetable to the animal kingdom, and to make them circulate from one to another. But laying these inquiries aside, in which we anticipate a little too much, let us, for the present, return to our tribes of plants.

The flowers that I have hitherto described to you are polypetalous. I ought perhaps to have begun with the regular monopetalous flowers, which have a much more simple structure, but it was this very simplicity that discouraged me. They constitute rather a great nation than a single tribe, so that to comprehend them all under one common mark, we must employ characters so general and so vague that while we seem to say something, in effect we scarcely say anything. It is better to confine ourselves within narrower bounds, which we can mark out with more precision.

Among the irregular monopetalous flowers, there is a tribe whose physiognomy is so marked that we distinguish the members of it easily by their air. It is that to whose flowers (Linnaeus) has given the name of ringent, because they are cut into two lips, the opening of which, whether natural or produced by a slight compression of the fingers, gives them the air of a gaping mouth. This tribe is divided into two branches: one of labiate or ringent flowers, properly so called, and the other of personate or masked flowers: the Latin word *persona* signifying a mask, certainly a very fitting name for most people among us who put on personas.

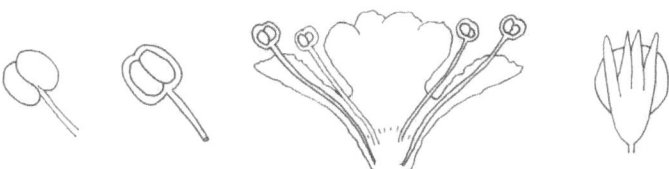

The character common to all the tribe is not only a monopetalous corol, cut into two lips, the upper one called the casque or helmet, the lower one the beard, but also four stamens, almost in the same row, distinguished into two pairs, one longer and the other shorter. The inspection of the object itself will explain these characters better to you than can be done in writing.

Let us begin with the labiate flowers. For an example I should willingly give you sage, which is common in almost all gardens: but the singular structure of its stamens, which has occasioned some botanists to separate it from the associates to which it naturally belongs, induces me to look for another instance in the dead nettles, especially in a species commonly called white nettle, but which botanists call white dead nettle, which notwithstanding its name has no affinity with nettles, properly so called, in terms of its fructification, except in the shape of the leaves. This plant is so common everywhere and continues so long in flower that it cannot be difficult for you to find it. Without stopping here to consider the elegant situation of the flowers, I will confine myself to their structure. The white dead nettle bears a monopetalous labiate corol, with the casque or upper lip arched in order to cover the rest of the flower, and particularly

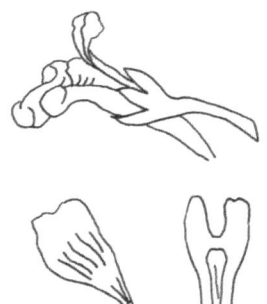

the stamens, which keep all four of them very close under cover of its roof. You will easily discern the longer pair and the shorter pair, and in the midst of them the style, of the same color but distinguished from them by being forked at the end, instead of bearing an anther like the stamens.

The beard or lower lip bends back and hangs down, so as to let you see the inside of the corol almost to the bottom. In this genus the lower lip is divided lengthwise in the middle, but that is not general in this tribe.

If you pull out the corol, you will take the stamens along with it, those being fastened by the filaments to that and not to the receptacle, whereon only the pistil will remain. In examining how the stamens are fastened in other flowers, we find them generally attached to the corol in monopetalous, and to the receptacle, or calyx, in polypetalous flowers: so that in the latter case, one may take away the petals without the stamens. From this observation we have an elegant, easy, and pretty certain rule to know whether a corol consists of one piece or several, when it is difficult, as it sometimes is, to be certain of it immediately.

The corol, when pulled off, is open at bottom because it was fastened to the receptacle, so as to leave a circular opening by which the pistil and what surrounds it may grow up within the tube. That which surrounds the pistil in this dead nettle, and all the labiate tribe, is the rudiment of the fruit, consisting of four embryos, which become four seeds that are naked.

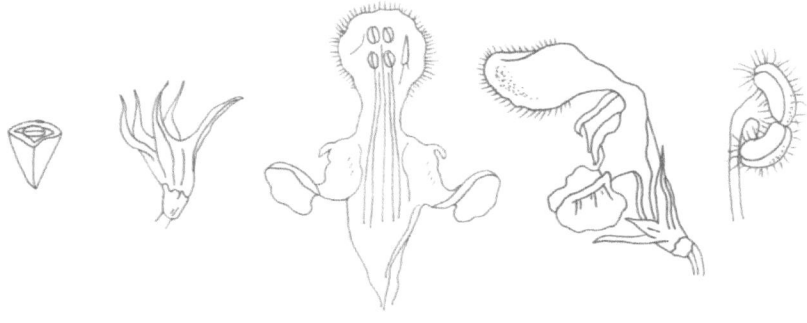

That is, without any (pericarp or) covering (the monophyllous calyx divided into five segments serving this purpose), so that the seeds, when they are tripe, are detached and fall to the ground separately. This is the character of the labiate flowers.

The other branch or section, which is that of the personate flowers, is distinguished from the former: first in having the two lips not usually open, or gaping, but closed and joined, as you may see in the snapdragon, a flower not uncommon in gardens, or for want of that in the toadflax, a yellow flower with a spur, so common in the country at this season. But a more precise and certain character is that instead of having four naked seeds at the bottom of the calyx, like the labiate flowers, these have a capsule or case enclosing the seeds and not opening until they are ripe, in order to disperse them. To these characters we may add that the greater part of the labiate plants are either strong smelling and aromatic, such as marjoram, thyme, wild thyme, basil, mint, hyssop, lavender, etc., or else strong smelling and stinking, such as the dead nettles, hedge nettle, catmint, black horehound, etc. Some few having only little or no smell, as bugle, self-heal, and hooded willow herb.

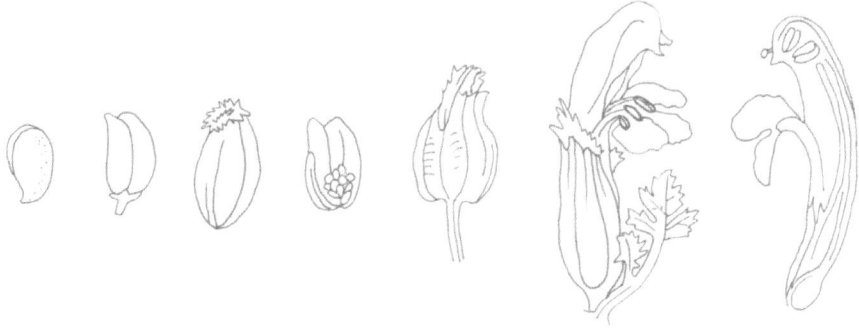

Whereas most of the plants with personate flowers are not odorous, such as snapdragons, toadflax, eyebright, lousewort, yellow rattle, broomrape, ivy-leaved toadflax, round-leaved toadflax, foxglove, etc. I know of none that have a strong smell in this branch but the scrophularia, or figwort, which smells strong without being aromatic. Here I am not able to name any but such plants as may perhaps be unknown to you, but you will gradually get acquainted with them, and whenever you see them you will be able by yourself to determine what class they belong to. I wish you would try to settle the branch or section by its physiognomy, and that you would exercise yourself in judging at sight whether a flower is labiate or personate. The exterior form of the corol may suffice to guide you in this choice, which you may verify afterward by pulling out the corol and looking at the bottom of the calyx; for, if you have judged right, the flower that you have named labiate will show you four naked seeds, and that which you have named personate will show you a pericarp: the contrary would prove that you were mistaken, and by a second examination of the same plant, you would prevent a like mistake another time. Here, dear cousin, is business cut out for several walks. I shall not fail to provide something for those that will succeed.

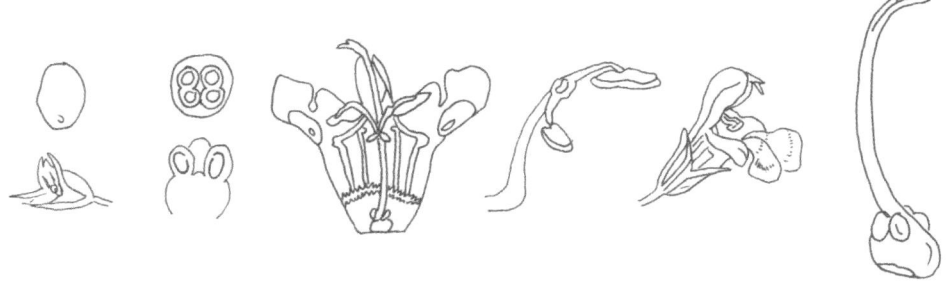

# LETTER V

Of Umbellate Plants • July 16, 1772

Comfort yourself, my good cousin, for not having detected the glands in the cruciform flowers. Great botanists, and quick-sighted ones too, have not been more happy. Tournefort himself makes no mention of them. They are very visible in but few genera, though we find vestiges of them in almost all, and it is by analyzing some of the cruciform flowers and always observing inequalities in the receptacle, and then examining these inequalities, that we find out that these glands belong to most of the genera, and suppose therefore by analogy that they exist in the others, where we do not distinguish them.

I comprehend that you may not be pleased at taking so much pains without knowing the names of the plants that you examine. But I own fairly that it did not enter into my plan to spare you that little chagrin. It is pretended that botany is merely a science of words, which only exercises the memory and teaches the names of plants. For my part I know not any reasonable study that is a mere science of words, and to which of these shall we give the name of botanist to him who has a name or a phrase ready when he sees a plant, but without knowing any thing of its structure, or to him who, being well acquainted with this structure, is ignorant nevertheless of the arbitrary name that the plant has in this or that country? If we give our children nothing but an amusing employment, we lose the best half of our design, which is, at the same time that we amuse them, to exercise their understandings and to accustom them to attention. Before we teach them to name what they see, let us begin by teaching them how to see. This science, which is forgotten in all sorts of education, should make the most important part of it. I can never repeat it often enough; teach them not to pay themselves in words, or to think they know anything of what is merely laid up in their memory.

| ATLAS OF ELEMENTARY BOTANY

However, not to play the rogue with you too much, I give you the names of some plants with which you may easily verify my descriptions, by causing them to be shown you. For instance, if you cannot find a white dead nettle when you are reading the analysis of the labiate or ringent flowers, you have nothing to do but to send to an herborist for it fresh gathered, to apply my description to the flower, and then having examined the other parts of the plant, in the manner that I shall hereafter point out, you will be infinitely better acquainted with the white dead nettle than the herborist who furnished you with it will ever be during his whole life; in a little time, however, we shall learn how to do without the herborist: but first we must finish the examination of our tribes. And now I come to the fifth, which at this time is in full fructification.

Figure to yourself a long stem, pretty straight, with leaves placed alternately upon it, generally cut fine, and embracing at the base branches that grow from their alae. From the upper part of this stem, as from a center, grow several pedicles or rays, which, spreading circularly and regularly like the ribs of an umbrella, crown the stem with a kind of basin, more or less open.

Sometimes these rays leave a fort of void in the middle and represent, in that case, more exactly the hollow of a basin: sometimes also this middle is furnished with other rays that are shorter, which, rising less obliquely, form with the others nearly the figure of a half sphere with the convex side uppermost.

Each of these rays is terminated not by a flower but by another set of smaller rays, crowning each of the former exactly as the first crown the stem.

Here then are two similar and successive orders: one of large rays, terminating the stem, and another of smaller rays, like the others, each of them terminating the great ones.

The rays of the little umbels are not further subdivided, but each of them is the pedicle to a little flower, of which we shall speak presently.

If you can frame an idea of the figure that I have just described, you will understand the disposition of the flowers in the tribe of umbelliferous or umbellate plants: *umbella* being the Latin word for an umbrella.

Though this regular disposition of the fructification be striking and sufficiently constant in all the umbellate plants, it is not that, however, that constitutes the character of the tribe. This is taken from the structure of the flower itself, which must therefore be described.

But it is expedient, for the sake of greater clearness, to give you in this place a general distinction with regard to the relative disposition of the flower and fruit in all plants, a distinction that extremely facilitates their methodical arrangement, whatever system you adopt for that purpose.

The greater number of plants, such as the pink, for instance, have the germ enclosed within the flower; these are called inferior flowers, as in enclosing or being below the germ.

Many, however, have the germ placed below the flower, as in the rose; for the hip, which is the fruit of it, is that green tumid body that you see under the calyx, and this with the corol crowns the germ and does not envelop it, as in the former case: such are called superior flowers, as in being above the germ. One could think of more-Gallicized terms, but it appears advantageous to me to always present you with the closest names to those accepted in botany, so that you be able, without the need to learn either Latin or Greek, to understand well enough the vocabulary of this science, which pedantically draws on these two languages, as if, to understand plants, it were necessary to first become a knowledgeable grammarian.

Tournefort expressed the same distinction in different terms: in the case of the inferior flower, he says that the pistil becomes the fruit; in the case of the superior flower, he says that the calyx becomes the fruit. This manner of expressing oneself may be as clear but is certainly lacking in accuracy. Whatever it may be, you have here an opportunity to educate, once the time has come, your young pupil in disentangling the same ideas expressed with thoroughly different terms.

I will tell you now that the umbellate plants have a superior flower above the fruit.

The corol has five petals, called regular, though frequently the two outermost petals of the flowers at the extremity of the umbel are larger than the three others. The form of these petals varies in the different genera, but it is usually cordate or heart shaped. They are very narrow next to the germ but gradually widen toward the end, which is emarginate, or slightly notched, or else they finish in a point, which, being folded back, gives the petal the air of being emarginate even though it looks pointed when folded back.

Between each petal is a stamen, and the anther generally standing out beyond the corol; the five stamens are more visible than the five petals. I make no mention here of the calyx, because it is not very distinct in the umbellate plants. (From the center of the flower arise two styles, each furnished with its stigma and sufficiently apparent; these are permanent, or continue after the petals and stamens fall off, to crown the fruit.)

The most usual figure of this fruit is an oblong oval; when ripe it opens in the middle and is divided into two naked seeds fastened to the pedicle, which, with an art that merits our admiration, divides in two, as well as the fruit, and keeps the seeds separately suspended until they fall.

All these proportions vary in the different genera, but this is the most common order. It requires a very attentive eye to accurately distinguish objects so minute without a glass, but they are so deserving of attention that we cannot regret the trouble of it.

This then is the proper character of the umbellate tribe.

A superior corol of five petals, five stamens, and two styles upon a naked fruit composed of two seeds growing together.

Whenever you find these characters united in one fructification, be sure that the plant is of this tribe, even though in other respects it should have nothing in its arrangement of the order before laid down. And if you should find all this order conformable to my description and see it, however, contradicted by the examination of the flower, be sure that you are deceived.

For instance, if it should happen that after having read my letter you should walk out and find an elder in flower, I am almost certain that at first sight you would say, here is an umbellate plant. In looking at it, you would find a large or universal umbel, a small or partial umbel, little white flowers, a superior corol, and five stamens; it is certainly an umbellate plant, say you. But let us see, let us take a flower.

In the first place, instead of five petals, I find a corol divided into five parts indeed, but all of one piece. Now, the flowers of umbellate plants are not monopetalous. There are five stamens, but I see no styles, and I more often see three stigmas than two; more often three seeds than two.

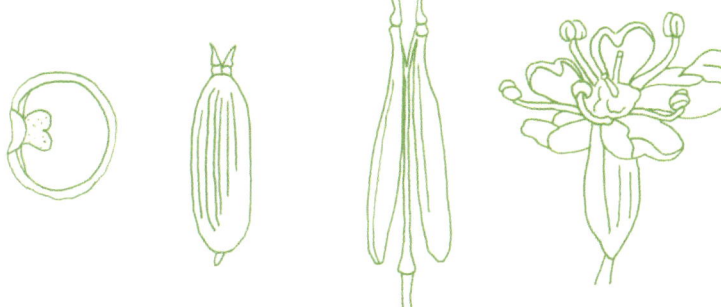

Now, the umbellate plants never have more or less than two stigmas, and two seeds to each flower. Last, the fruit of the elder is a soft berry, and that of the umbellate tribe dry and naked. The elder then is not an umbellate plant.

If now you go back and inspect with more accuracy the disposition of the flowers, you will see that the elder has the structure of the umbellate tribe only in appearance. Though the principal rays proceed from the same center, the smaller ones are irregular, and the flowers are born on a second subdivision: in short, the whole has not that order and regularity that we find in the umbellate plants. The arrangement of the flowers in the elder is called a cyme. Thus by making a blunder sometimes, we learn to see with more accuracy.

Eryngo, on the contrary, has little or nothing the air of an umbelliferous plant, and yet it is one, because it has all the characters of the fructification. Where does one find eryngo, you ask? Everywhere in the countryside, to the left and right of each road, every peasant may point it out to you, and (if you were by the seaside), you would easily know it by the bluish or sea-green color of the leaves, by their prickliness, and by the smooth, membranous consistence of them, like parchment.

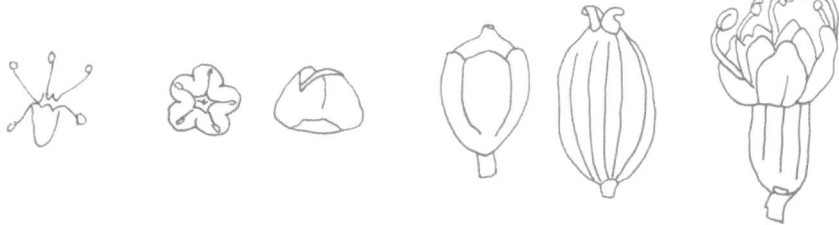

But this plant is uncommon in other situations, is rough and intractable, and has not beauty enough to make you amends for the wounds it will give you in examining it, and though it were ever so beautiful, my little cousin with her tender little fingers would soon be disgusted at handling so ill-humored a plant. The umbelliferous tribe is numerous and so natural that it is very difficult to distinguish the genera: they are relations, whom we often take for each other on account of their great resemblance. To assist us in distinguishing them, the principal differences are noticed, which are sometimes useful, but which we must not depend upon too much. The focus of the rays both in the larger or universal, and in the smaller or partial umbel, is not always naked; it is sometimes surrounded with small leaves. This set of small leaves or folioles is called involucre. When it is placed at the origin of the universal umbel, it is named the universal involucre, and when at the origin of the partial umbel, it is named the partial involucre. This gives rise to three sections of umbellate plants:

1. those that have both involucres
2. those that have partial involucres only
3. those that have neither

There seems to be a fourth division wanting of those that have an universal involucre only, but there is no genus that is constantly so.

Your astonishing progress, my dear cousin, and unwearied patience have emboldened me so much that, not regarding your sufferings, I have ventured to describe the umbellate plants without fixing your eyes upon any model, which must needs have rendered your attention much more fatiguing. I am certain, however, that, reading as you do, after you have looked over my letter once or twice, an umbellate plant in flower will not escape you, and at this season you cannot fail finding many, both in the gardens and the fields.

Most of them have their little flowers white. As the carrot, chervil, parsley, hemlock, fool's parsley, angelica, cow parsnip, water parsnip, burnet saxifrage, pignuts, cow weed, etc.

Some, such as fennel, dill, and parsnip, have yellow flower; there are some few with reddish flowers, but none of any other color.

Here, you will tell me, may be a good general notion of umbellate plants, but how will all this vague knowledge ensure me from confounding fool's parsley with true parsley or chervil, which you have mentioned altogether? The meanest kitchen maid will know more of this matter than we with all our learning. You are right. But, however, if we begin with observations in detail, we shall soon be overwhelmed with the number of them; our memory will abandon us and we shall be lost the first step we make in this vast region, whereas if we begin with knowing the great roads well, we shall seldom be lost in the bypaths and shall always find our way again without much trouble. Let us, however, admit an exception in favor of the utility of the object, and let us not expose ourselves, while we are analyzing the vegetable kingdom, to eat fool's parsley with our meat, or in our soup, through mere ignorance.

This plant, which is so common a weed in gardens, is of the umbellate tribe, as well as parsley and chervil. It has a white flower as well as they;[1] it is in the same section with the latter, among those that have the partial and not the universal involucre; it is so like them in its foliage that it is not easy to mark the difference in writing. But here follow characters sufficient to prevent you from being mistaken. You must consider these plants when they are all in flower; for in that state, only they have their proper character. The fool's parsley (*Aethusa cynapium*) has under every partial umbel an involucre of three narrow, long, pointed folioles, all placed on the outer part of the umbel and hanging down, whereas the folioles of the partial umbels in the chervil surround it entirely and grow equally on every side: and as to parsley, it has only a few short folioles, fine almost as hairs, each of them light in color and sparse and distributed indifferently at the base of both umbels.

When you are very certain of the fool's parsley in flower, you will confirm yourself in your judgment by slightly bruising and smelling its foliage, for the disagreeable venomous smell will no longer suffer you to confound it with parsley or chervil, both of which have rather a pleasant smell.

---

1. The flower of parsley is yellowish. But the flowers appear yellow in many of the umbellate plants, from the germ and anthers being so, though the corol is white.

Very certain at length, not to make a mistake, you will examine these three plants together and separately in every state, and in all their parts, especially in their foliage, which accompanies them more constantly than the flower, and by this examination compared and repeated, until you have acquired certainty at sight, you will be able to know and distinguish them without the least trouble. Thus does study bring us to the very door of practice, after which the latter confers the facility of knowing things.

Take breath, dear cousin, for this is an unconscionable letter, and yet I dare not promise you more discretion in the next; after that, however, we shall have nothing before us but a path bordered with flowers. You deserve a garland for the cheerfulness and perseverance with which you have condescended to followed me through these briars, without being discouraged at their thorns.

# LETTER VI

Of Compound Flowers • May 22, 1773

Though there is still, dear cousin, a great deal wanting to complete our idea of the five former tribes of plants, and I have not always known how to adapt my descriptions to the understanding of our young botanophile (amateur botanist), I flatter myself, however, that I have given you such an idea of them, as to enable you, after some months herborization, to render the (air), port (or habit), of each tribe familiar to you: so, that when you see a plant, you may conjecture nearly whether it belongs to one of these five tribes, and to which, provided always that by an analysis of the fructification, you afterward see whether you may not have been deceived in your conjecture. The umbellate plants, for instance, have thrown you into some embarrassment, from which, however, you may easily escape when you please, by means of the hints that I have subjoined to my descriptions. In short, carrots and parsnips are so common that nothing is easier in the middle of summer than for the gardener to send you one or other of them in flower out of the kitchen garden. Now, from the mere view of an umbel, and the plant that bears it, you must acquire so clear an idea of the umbellate tribe that you will rarely be deceived at first sight whenever you meet with one. This is all that I have hitherto pretended, for we have nothing to do yet with genera and species, and I repeat it once more that it is not the nomenclature of a parrot that I wish you to acquire, but a real science, and one of the most delightful sciences that it is possible to cultivate. I go on, therefore, to our sixth tribe before I take a more methodical road. It may perhaps at first embarrass you as much if not more than the umbellate plants. But my design at present is nothing more than to give you a general notion of it, especially since we still have plenty of time before the generality of these plants is in full flower, and the interval, well employed, will smooth those difficulties against which we have not strength to contend.

Take one of those little flowers that, at this season, cover all the pastures, and that everybody knows by the name of daisy. Look at it well, for by its appearance I am sure you will be surprised when I tell you that this flower, which is so small and delicate, is really composed of between two and three hundred other flowers, all of them perfect; that is, having each its corol, germ, pistil, stamens, and seed; in a word, as perfect in its species as a flower of the hyacinth or lily. Every one of those leaves that are white above and red underneath and form a kind of crown around the flower, appearing to be nothing more than little petals, are in reality so many true flowers, and also every one of those tiny yellow things that you see in the center and that at first you have perhaps taken for nothing but stamens are real flowers. If your fingers were already exercised in botanical dissections, and you were armed with a good glass and plenty of patience, I might convince you of the truth of this, but at present you must begin, if you please, by believing me on my word, for fear of fatiguing your attention upon atoms.

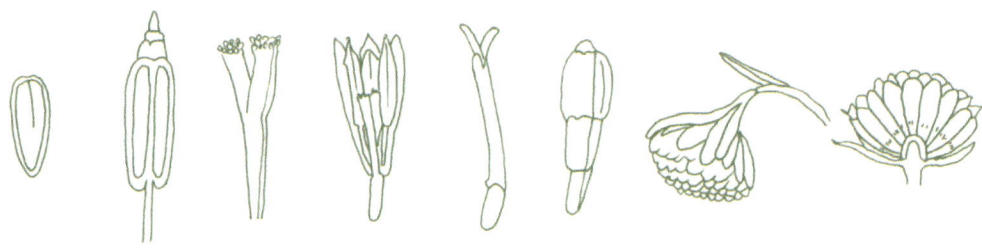

However, to put you at least in the way, pull out one of the white leaves from the flower; you will think at first that it is flat from one end to the other, but look carefully at the end by which it was fastened to the flower, and you will see that it is not flat, but round and hollow in form of a tube, and that a little thread ending in two horns issues from the tube; this thread is the forked style of the flower, which, as you now see, is flat only at top.

Now look at those little yellow things in the middle of the flower, which, as I have told you, are all so many flowers; if the flower be sufficiently advanced, you will see several of them open in the middle and even cut into several parts.

These are monopetalous corols, which expand, and a glass will easily discover in them the pistil, and even the anthers with which it is surrounded. Commonly, the yellow florets toward the center are still rounded and closed. These however are flowers like the others, but not yet open, for they expand successively from the edge inward. This is enough to show you by the eye the possibility that all these small affairs, both white and yellow, may be so many distinct flowers, and this is a constant fact.

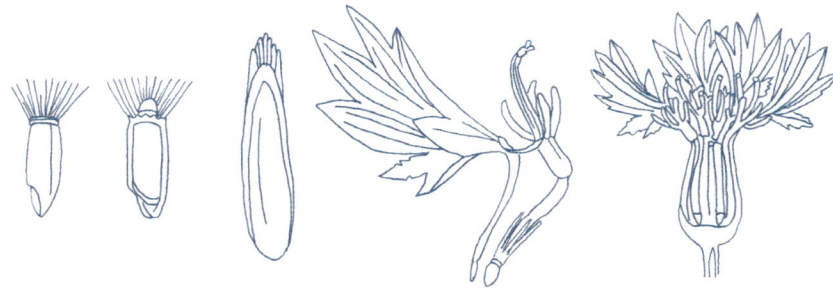

You perceive, nevertheless, that all these little flowers are pressed, and enclosed in a calyx, which is common to them all and is that of the daisy. In considering, then, the whole daisy as one flower, we give it a very significant name when we call it a compound flower. Now, there are many genera and species of flowers formed, like the daisy, of an assemblage of other small flowers, contained in a common calyx. This is what constitutes the sixth tribe of which I proposed to treat; namely, that of the compound flowers.

Let us begin by avoiding all ambiguity with regard to the word "flower," which we may do in the current case by restraining it to the compound flower and giving the name of floscules or florets to the little component flowers, but in the midst of this verbal precision, let us not forget that each of these florets is a genuine flower.

You have observed two sort of florets in the daisy: the yellow ones, which occupy the middle or disk of the flower, and the little white tongues or straps, which surround them.

The former are something like the flowers of the lily of the valley, or hyacinth, in miniature, and the latter bear some resemblance to those of the honeysuckle.

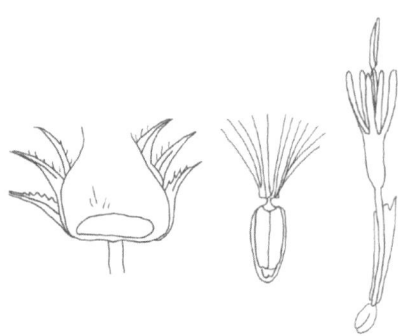

We shall leave to the first the name of florets, and to distinguish the second we shall call them semiflorets: for in reality they have a little the air of monopetalous flowers gnawed off on one side, and having scarcely half the corol remaining.

These two sorts of florets are combined in the compound flowers in such a manner as to divide the whole tribe into three sections, very distinct from each other.

The first section consists of those that are entirely composed of semiflorets, both in the middle and circumference; these are called semiflosculous flowers, and the whole is always of one color, which is generally yellow. Such is the common dandelion, the lettuce (and sow thistle), the succory (and endive), which have blue flowers, the scorzonera, salsafy, etc.

The second section comprehends the flosculous flowers, or such as are composed of florets only: these are also commonly of one color, such as immortal flowers, burdock, wormwood, mugwort, thistles, and artichoke, which is nearly allied to them; it is the calyx of this that we suck and the receptacle that we eat, while it is yet young, before the flower opens or is even formed. The choke, which we take out of the middle, is an assemblage of florets that are beginning to be formed and are separated from each other by long hairs affixed in the receptacle.

The third section is of flowers composed of both these. They are always so arranged that the florets occupy the center of the flower, and the semiflorets the circumference, as you have seen in the daisy. The flowers of this section are called radiate. Botanists have given the name of ray to the set of semiflorets that compose the circumference, and of disk to the area or center of the flower occupied by the florets. This name of disk is sometimes given to the surface of the receptacle in which all the florets and semiflorets are affixed.

In the radiate flowers, the disk is often of one color, and the ray of another; there are, however, genera and species in which both are alike.

Let us endeavor now to fix in your mind an idea of a compound flower. The common clover is in blow at this season; the flower is purple: if you should take one in hand, seeing so many little flowers assembled, you might be tempted to take the whole for a compound flower. You would, however, be mistaken; in what? say you. Why in supposing that an assemblage of many little flowers is sufficient to constitute a compound flower: whereas, besides this, one or two parts of the fructification must be common to them all, so that everyone must have a part in it, and no one have its own separately: these two parts in common are the calyx and receptacle. The flower of the clover, indeed, or rather the group of flowers, which has the appearance of being but one flower, seems at first to be placed upon a sort of calyx, but remove this pretended calyx a little and you will perceive that it does not belong to the flower, but that it is fastened below it to the pedicle that bears it. This, then, is a calyx only in appearance, but in reality it belongs to the foliage, not to the flower, and this supposed compound flower is only an assemblage of very small leguminous or papilionaceous flowers, each of which has its distinct calyx, and they have nothing common to them but their being fastened to the same pedicle. Vulgarly, all this is taken for one flower; it is a false idea, however, or if we must look upon it as such, we must not at least call it a compound, but an aggregate or capitate flower, or a head of flowers, and these terms are sometimes so applied by botanical writers.

This, dear cousin, is the most simple and natural notion I can give you of this numerous class of compound flowers, and the three sections into which it is subdivided. I now come to the structure of the fructifications particular to this class, and this perhaps will bring us to determine the character of it with more precision.

The most essential part of a compound flower is the receptacle, upon which are placed first the florets and semiflorets and then the seeds that succeed them. This receptacle, which forms a disk of some extent, makes the center of the calyx, as you may see in the dandelion, which we will here take as an instance. The calyx in this tribe is commonly divided into several parts, down to the base, so that it may close, open again, and turn back, as it does during the progress of the fructification, without being torn. The calyx of the dandelion is formed of two rows of folioles, inserted into each other, and the folioles of the outer row turn back and curl downward toward the pedicle, while the folioles of the inner row continue straight, to surround and hold in the semiflorets composing the flower.

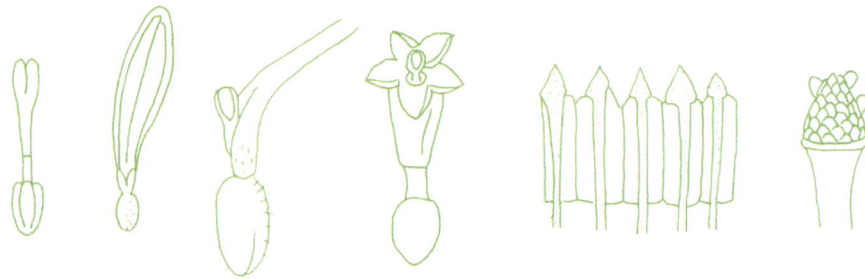

One of the most common forms also of the calyx in this class is the imbricate, or that which is made up of several rows of folioles, laying over each other like tiles on a roof. The artichoke, bluebottle, knapweeds, and scorzoneras may serve as instances of imbricate calyxes.

The florets and semiflorets enclosed within the calyx are placed very thickly upon the disk or receptacle in form of a quincunx, or the checks upon a chessboard. Sometimes they touch each other without anything interposed between them; sometimes they are separated by partitions of hairs, or small scales, which continue fast to the receptacle after the seeds are fallen. You are now in the way to observe the differences of calyxes and receptacles: we will go on then to the structure of florets and semiflorets, beginning with the former.

A floret is a monopetalous flower, commonly regular, with the corol divided at top into four or five parts. The five filaments of the stamens are fastened to the tube of this corol: they are united at top into a little round tube, which surrounds the pistil, and this tube is the five anthers united circularly into one body. This union of the anthers, according to (modern) botanists, forms the essential character of compound flowers and belongs to their florets only, exclusively of all others. If therefore you find several flowers upon the same disk, as in the scabiouses and teasels, unless the anthers are united in a tube around the pistil and the corol stands upon one naked seed, such flowers are not florets, nor do they form a compound flower.

On the contrary, whenever you find in a single flower the anthers thus united, and a superior corol on a single seed, this flower, though sole, is a genuine floret and belongs to the compound tribe, for it is better thus to take the character from a precise structure than from a deceitful appearance.

The pistil has the style generally longer than the floret, above which it rises through the tube formed by the anthers. It is most frequently terminated at top by a forked stigma, the two curling horns of which are very visible. The pistil does not rest upon the receptacle any more than the floret, but both upon the germ, which serves them as a base, and grows and lengthens as the floret withers, becoming in time a longish seed, remaining fastened to the receptacle until it is ripe: then it falls, if it be naked, or the wind wafts it to a distance if it be crowned with an egret of feathers or hairs, and the receptacle remains quite naked in some genera but is furnished with scales or hairs in others.

The structure of the semiflorets is like that of the florets; the stamens, the pistil, and the seed are arranged almost in the same manner, and only in the radiate flowers are there many genera, wherein the semiflorets of the ray are apt to be abortive, either because they have no stamens or because those that they have are barren and have not the power to fertilize the germ: in such cases, the flower seeds only by the florets in the middle.

In the whole compound class, the seed is always sessile; that is, it bears immediately upon the receptacle without any intermediate pedicle.

But there are seeds in which the down or egret that crowns them is sessile, and others in which it is fastened to the seed by a pedicle. You understand that the use of this down is to spread the seeds about to a distance, by giving the air more hold upon them.

To these irregular imperfect descriptions I should add that the calyx generally has the property of opening when the flower expands, of closing when the florets fall off, in order to confine the young seed, and to hinder it from falling before it is ripe, and last, of opening again and turning quite back to give a larger area to the seeds, which increase in size as they grow ripe. You must have often seen the dandelion in this state, when children gather it to blow off the down that forms a ball around the reverted calyx.

To understand this class well, you must follow the flowers from before their expansion to the full maturity of the fruit, and in this succession you will see transformations and a chain of wonders that will keep every sensible mind that observes them in a continual admiration. One flower proper for these observations is the sunflower, which one frequently encounters in vineyards and gardens. The sunflower, as you will see, is radiate, as are also oxeye (Chinese aster, and many others), which are the ornament of the borders in autumn. I have already said that there are thistles[2] for the flosculous, and scorzonera and dandelion for the semiflosculous flowers. All these are large enough to be dissected and studied with the naked eye, without fatiguing yourself too much.

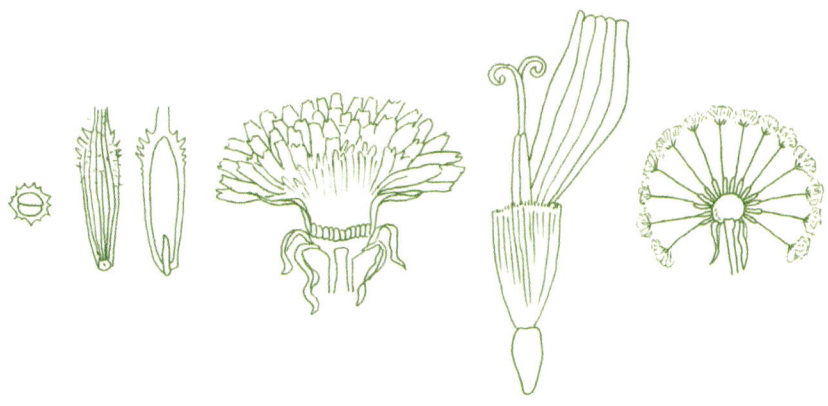

I will not trouble you at present anymore upon the tribe or class of compound flowers. I tremble already at having abused your patience too much by details that would have been clearer if I had known how to make them shorter, but it is impossible for me to avoid the difficulty arising from the smallness of objects. Adieu, dear cousin.

---

2. One must pay attention so as not to confuse it with the Indian or draper's teasel, which is not a true thistle.

# LETTER VII

Of Fruit Trees

Here, dear cousin, you have the names of those plants that you sent me last. I have put a mark of interrogation to those that I had any doubt of, because you had not taken care to put the leaves with the flower, and they are often necessary to determine the species, especially to so slender a botanist as I am. When you arrive at Fourriere you will find most of the fruit trees in flower, and I remember you requested some directions from me upon this article. At present I can give you only some hints upon the subject, because I am very busy, and yet I would not have you lose the season for this examination.

You must not, my dear friend, give more importance to botany than it really has; it is a study of pure curiosity and has no other real use than that, which a thinking sensible being may deduce from the observation of nature and the wonders of the universe.

Man has changed the nature of many things to convert them better to his own use; in that he is not to be blamed, but then it is nevertheless true that he has often disfigured them, and that when he thinks he is studying nature in the works of his own hands, he is frequently mistaken. This error is found above all in civil society, but it has a place also in gardens. The double flowers, which we admire so much in our borders and beds, are but monsters, deprived of the power of producing their like, a power with which nature has endowed every organized being. Fruit trees are somewhat in the same case, by being ingrafted; you may plant the pips or seeds of pears and apples of the best sorts, but they will produce nothing but wildlings. To know then the pear and the apple of nature, you must look for them not in orchards, but in woods.

The flesh or pulp is not so large and succulent, but the seeds ripen better and multiply more, and the trees are vastly bigger and more vigorous. But I am entering on a subject that would carry me too far: let us return to the orchard. Our fruit trees, though ingrafted, preserve all the botanical characters that distinguish them, and it is by an attentive consideration of these characters, as well as by the transformation of the graft, that we ascertain there being but one species of pear, for instance, under a thousand different names, by which the shape and taste of their fruits have caused them to be distinguished into so many pretended species, which are, at bottom, but varieties: nay more, the pear and apple are only two sorts or species of the same kind or genus, and their only characteristic difference is that the stalk of the apple enters into a hollow in the fruit, and that of the pears is fastened to the narrow part of a fruit a little lengthened out. In the same manner the different sorts of wild, sour, and sweet cherries are nothing but varieties of the same species; all the plums are but one species of plum; nay, the genus of prunus or plum contains three principal species; the plum properly so called, the cherry, and the apricot, which also is only a species of plum.

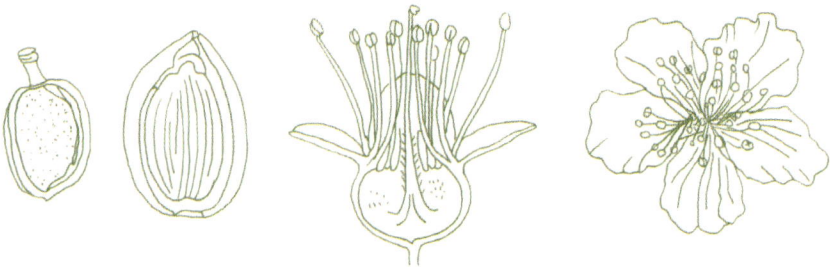

Thus when the learned Linnaeus, in dividing the genus into its species, has enumerated the domestic plum, the plum cherry, and the plum apricot, ignorant people have laughed at him, but observers have admired the justness of his arrangement. I ought to rush; I am in a hurry.

The fruit trees belong mostly to a numerous tribe, which has a character not difficult to seize; the stamens, which are many in number, instead of arising from the receptacle are fastened to the calyx, either immediately or with the corol, which is polypetalous and consists commonly of five petals. The following are characters of some of the principal genera.

The pear, comprehending also the apple and the quince, has the calyx monophyllous, divided into five segments; the corol of five petals is fastened to the calyx, about twenty stamens, all fastened likewise to the calyx. The germ or ovary is inferior, and there are five styles. The fruit (as everybody knows) is fleshy and has five cells containing the seeds etc.

The genus plum, comprehending the apricot and cherry (as was before observed) and also the laurel, has the calyx, corol, and stamens nearly as in the pear. But the germ is superior, or within the corol, and there is but one style. The fruit is rather watery than fleshy and contains a stone etc.

# LETTER VII

The genus almond, including the peach (and nectarine), is almost like the plum, but the germ has a down upon it, and the fruit (which everybody knows) is succulent in the peach and dry in the almond and encloses a hard stone, which is rough and full of cavities etc.

All this is very roughly sketched out, but I hope it contains enough to amuse you for the present. Adieu, dear cousin.

# LETTER VIII

Of Making a Hortus Siccus, or Herbarium • April 11, 1773

I thank the heavens, dear cousin, that you are finally recovered. Yet, your silence has given me cause for concern. Among worries of this kind, nothing is more cruel than silence, since it renders everything worse. But all this is already forgotten, and I only rejoice in your recovery. The onset of the warmer months and the pleasure of successfully fulfilling the sweetest and most respectable of duties will soon strengthen you, and you will feel the temporary absence of your husband less keenly amid the dear guarantees of his attachment and the continuous care these demand of you.

The earth (dear cousin) begins to put on its green robe, the trees to bud, the flowers to open; some are even already past; an instant of delay would be the loss of a whole year for botany: I proceed then without further preamble.

I fear we have hitherto treated our subject in too abstract a way, by not having applied our ideas to determinate objects: it is a fault that I have been guilty of, especially in the umbellate tribe. If I had begun by setting one of them before your eyes, I should have spared you a very fatiguing application to an imaginary object, as well as a very difficult description to myself, and such as a single look would have supplied. Unfortunately, at a distance to which the law of necessity restrains me, I am not able to deliver the objects into your hand, but provided each of us can but see with the same eyes, we shall understand one another very well when we relate what we see. The whole difficulty is that the indication must come from you, for to send you dried plants from hence would be doing nothing. To know a plant well, you must begin with seeing it growing.

A hortus siccus, by which Latin term we call a collection of dried plants, may serve to put us in mind of the plants we have once known, but gives us only a poor knowledge of those that we have never seen before. You therefore must send me such plants as you wish to know and have gathered yourself, and it is my business to name, class, and describe them until, by comparative ideas become familiar to your eyes and your understanding, you arrive at classing, ranging, and naming, by yourself, those that you see for the first time: and this is the science that distinguishes the true botanist from the mere herborist or nomenclator. My design then here is to teach you how to prepare, dry, and preserve plants, or specimens of plants, in such a manner as that they may be easily known and determined. In a word, I propose to you to begin a hortus siccus. Here is a deal of business preparing at a distance for our little botanist: for at present, and for some time to come, the address of your fingers must supply the weakness of hers.

First, here is some provision to be made; namely, five or six quires of gray paper, and almost as many of white, of the same bigness, pretty strong and well sized, without which the specimens would rot in the gray paper, the plants or at least the flowers would lose their color, and this, of all the parts, is that by which they are most easily known, and which it is most pleasant to see in a collection of dried plants.

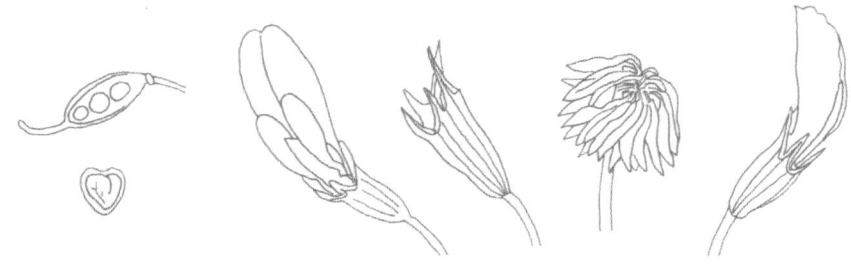

It was also to be wished that you had a press of the same size with your paper, or at least two pieces of board well planed, between which you may keep your papers and specimens, pressed by stones or any other weight with which you may load the upper plank. When you have made these preparations, you must observe the following rules in order to prepare your plants so as to preserve them and know them again.

The precise time to gather your plant is when it is in full flower, or rather when some of the flowers begin to fall, to give place to the fruit, which begins to make its appearance. It is at this time, when all parts of the fructification are visible, that you must endeavor to gather the plant in order to dry it.

Small plants may be taken whole with their roots, which must be brushed so that no earth may remain. If the earth is wet, it must either be dried, so that it may be brushed, or else the root must be washed, but in this case you should wipe it well and dry it before you put it into the papers, without which it would infallibly rot and injure the plants near it. You need not, however, preserve the roots, unless they have some remarkable singularities, for in most plants the branching fibrous roots are so alike that it is not worth the trouble. Nature, which has done so much for elegance and ornament in the form and color of plants, in whatever strikes our sight, has destined the roots entirely to useful functions, because being concealed within the earth, to give them an agreeable structure, would have been to hide the light under a bushel.

Trees and all great plants can be had only by specimens: but then that specimen should be so well chosen as to contain all the constituent parts of the genus and species, so that it may suffice to know and determine the plant whence it is taken. It is not sufficient that all the parts of the fructification are distinguishable, which would be enough to determine the genus, but the character of the foliation and ramification also must be sufficiently visible; that is, the origin and form of the leaves and branches, and even as much as may be some portion of the main stem itself, for as you will see in the sequel, all this serves to distinguish the species of the same genus, which are perfectly alike in the flower and fruit. If the branches are too thick, they may be made thinner by cutting them with a sharp knife or penknife nicely underneath, as much as may be without cutting and mutilating the leaves. There are botanists who have the patience to slit the bark and raw the wood out so nicely that when the bark is united again, the branch seems to be entire though the wood is gone: by which means there are none of those inequalities and bumps, which spoil and disfigure a collection and give a bad form to the plants. Where the flowers and leaves do not come out at the same time or grow too far distant from each other, you will take a little branch in flower and another in leaf, and placing them together on the same leaf of your book, you thus have before you different parts of the same plant, sufficient to give you a complete knowledge of it. As to plants where you find only the leaves, the flower being either past or not yet come, you must wait with patience until they show their faces to be fully acquainted with them.

A plant being no more certainly to be known by its foliage than a man by his clothes.

Such is the choice that you should make in what you gather: you must have a choice also as to the time in which you do it. Plants gathered in the morning before the dew is off, or in the evening when it is damp, or in the daytime when it is wet will not keep. You must absolutely choose a dry season, and even then, the driest and hottest time of the day, which in summer is between eleven in the morning and five in the afternoon. Even then, if you find the least moisture on them, you must not take them, for they will certainly not keep.

When you have gathered your specimens, you must bring them home as soon as you can, quite dry, to put and arrange them in your papers. For this purpose you lay down at least one sheet of gray paper, upon this half a sheet of white paper, and then your plant, taking great care that all the parts of it, especially the leaves and flowers, are well opened and laid out in their natural situation. If the plant is a little withered, without being too much so, it will generally spread out better upon the paper with the fingers and thumb. But there are rebellious plants that start up on one side while you are arranging them on the other. To prevent this inconvenience, I have leads, halfpence, and farthings that I place upon those parts that I have just put in order while I am arranging the rest, so that when I have finished, my plant is almost covered with these pieces, which keep it in its proper situation.

Then you place another half sheet of white paper upon the first, pressing it with your hand, to keep the plant in the position you have given it, bringing your left hand that presses gradually forward, and at the same time taking away the leads etc. with your right, then put another two sheets of gray paper upon the second white sheet, all the while pressing the plant, lest it lose the position you have given it: upon the gray paper, place another half sheet of white, as before; upon this, another plant arranged and covered like the former, until you have placed your whole harvest, which ought not to be too numerous at once, both that your task may not be too laborious and that your paper may not contract too much humidity during the drying, which would infallibly spoil your plants unless you hastened to change the papers with the same attention as before; this, however, is what you must do from time to time, until your specimens have taken their bent and are all very dry.

Your pile of plants and papers, thus arranged, must be put into the press, without which your plants will not be flat and even; some are for pressing them more, others less; experience will teach you this, as well as how often the papers should be changed, without taking unnecessary pains. Last, when your plants are quite dry, put each of them separately into a sheet of paper, one upon another, without other papers between, for which there is no occasion, and you will thus begin a hortus siccus, which will continually increase with your knowledge and at length contain the history of all the vegetation of the country. Take care always to keep your collection very close and a little pressed, without which the plants, however dry they might be, will attract the humidity of the air, and again get out of form.

Now, the use of all these pains is to arrive at a knowledge of each particular plant, and to understand one another well when we talk of them.

For this purpose you must gather two specimens of each plant: one larger to be kept, the other smaller to send me. You must number them carefully, so that both great and little specimen shall always have the same number. When you have a dozen or two of species thus dried, you will send them to me in a little parcel by the first opportunity. I will send you back their names and descriptions; by means of the numbers, you will know them in your collection, and after that in their natural state, wherein, I presume, you first examined them. This is the certain way to make as secure and rapid a progress as you can, at a distance from your guide.

P.S. I forgot to tell you that the same papers may serve over and over again, provided you take care to air and dry them well. I should also add here that your hortus siccus must be kept in the driest part of the house, and rather on the first than the ground floor.

# FRAGMENTS FOR A DICTIONARY OF BOTANICAL TERMS

## Introduction

The principal misfortune of botany is that from its very birth, it has been looked upon merely as a part of medicine. This was the reason why everybody was employed in finding or supposing virtues in plants, while the knowledge of plants themselves was totally neglected: for how could the same man make such long and repeated excursions as so extensive a study demands, and at the same time apply himself to the sedentary labors both of the laboratory and attendance upon the sick, which are the only methods of ascertaining the nature of vegetable substances and their effects upon the human body? This false idea of botany, for a long time, almost confined the study of it to medicinal plants and reduced the vegetable chain to a small number of interrupted links. Even these were ill-studied, because only the substance was attended to, and not the organization. How indeed could they be much interested in the organic structure of a substance of which they had no other idea but as a thing to be pounded in a mortar? Plants were searched for only to find remedies; it was simples, not vegetables, that were looked after. This was very right, it will be said; may be so. Hence, nevertheless it follows that if men were ever so well acquainted with remedies, they were very ignorant of plants, and this is all that I have here advanced.

Botany was nothing; there was no such study, and they who plumed themselves most upon their knowledge of vegetables had no idea of their structure or of the vegetable economy. Everybody knew by sight five or six plants in his neighborhood, to which he gave names at random, enriched with wonderful virtues, which he took it in his head they possessed, and each of these plants, changed into an universal panacea, was alone sufficient to render all mankind immortal.

These plants, transformed into balsams and ointments, quickly disappeared and soon made room for others, to which newcomers, in order to distinguish themselves, attributed the same effects. Sometimes it was a new plant, decorated with ancient virtues: sometimes old plants, under new names, sufficed to enrich new quacks. These plants had a different vulgar name in every province, and they who pointed them out for their drugs at most gave them only those names by which they were known on the spot where they lived: thus, when their recipes traveled into other countries, it was no longer known what plant they spoke of; everybody substituted another after his own fancy, without regarding anything else, but giving it the same name. Such is the whole art that the Myrepsuses, the Hildegardises, the Suardi, the Villanovae, and the rest of the doctors of that time employed in the study of those plants that they treat of, and it would be difficult perhaps for anybody to know one of them by the names or descriptions that they have given them. Instead of searching for plants where they grew, men studied them only in Pliny and Dioscorides, and there is nothing so frequent in the authors of those times as to find them denying the existence of a plant for no other reason but because Dioscorides has not mentioned it. These learned plants, however, must be found in nature in order to make use of them according to the precepts of their master. They bestirred themselves therefore; they set themselves to search, to observe, to conjecture and made every effort to find, in the plant that they chose, the characters described in their author, and since translators, commentators, and practitioners seldom agreed in their choice, twenty names were given to the same plant, and the same name to twenty plants, every man maintaining that his own was the true one, and that all the rest, not being that of Dioscorides, ought to be proscribed.

From this conflict indeed it followed at length that more-careful research was done, and some good observations that deserved not to be forgotten, but at the same time such a chaos of nomenclature that the physicians and herborists no longer understood each other: there was no possibility of communicating their mutual lights, nothing remained but disputes of words and names, and even every useful inquiry and description was lost for want of being able to decide what plant each author had spoken of.

Real botanists, however, began to be formed, such as Clusius, Cordus, Caesalpinus, and Gesner; good and instructive books on this subject began to be published, in which already appeared some traces of method. And it has certainly been a loss that these pieces have become useless and unintelligible by the mere discordance of names. But these authors, beginning to unite species and separate genera according to their own manner of observing the habit and apparent structure, occasioned new inconveniences and a fresh obscurity, because each author, regulating his nomenclature by his own method, created new genera or separated old ones as the characters of his own required. So that genera and species were so jumbled together, as to leave scarcely any plant without as many names as authors who described it, which made the study of the nomenclature as tedious, and often more difficult, than that of the plants themselves.

At length, two illustrious brothers appeared who alone have done more for the advancement of botany than all the rest together who preceded, and even followed, them, until Tournefort.

Rare geniuses!, whose vast knowledge and solid labors, consecrated to botany, render them worthy of that immortality that they have acquired. For until this part of natural history falls into oblivion, the names of John and Caspar Bauhin will live along with it in the memory of mankind.

Each of these men undertook a universal history of plants, but what more immediately relates to our present purpose is that they each undertook to join to it a synonymy, or exact list of the names that every plant bore in all the writers who preceded them. This labor became absolutely necessary to enable us to reap any advantage of their observations, for without that it was almost impossible to follow and distinguish every plant among so many names.

The eldest in a manner executed this undertaking in three volumes in folio, printed after his death, and he has given such just descriptions of the plants that we are rarely deceived in his synonyms.

The brother's plan was yet more extensive, as appears by the first volume that he published, and from which we may judge the immensity of the whole work if he had found time to execute it; however, excepting this volume, we have no more than the titles of the rest in his pinax, and this pinax, the product of forty years labor, is still the guide to all those who study this subject and wish to consult ancient authors.

The nomenclature of the Bauhins was formed only from the titles of their chapters, and these titles usually comprising several words; hence came the custom of giving, as the names of plants, nothing but long, ambiguous phrases, which made this nomenclature not only tedious and embarrassing, but pedantic and ridiculous.

# INTRODUCTION

I own there might have been some advantage in this, provided their phrases had been better constructed, but being composed indifferently of the names of places whence the plants came, of persons who sent them, and even of other plants to which they fancied them to bear some similitude, these phrases were sources of new embarrassment and fresh doubts because the knowledge of one plant required that of several others to which the phrase referred, and whose names were not better determined than its own.

In the meantime, distant voyages were incessantly enriching botany with new treasures, and while the old names already overloaded the memory, it was necessary to invent new ones incessantly for the new plants that were discovered. Lost in the immense labyrinth, the botanists were obliged to seek a thread to extricate themselves from it; they attached themselves therefore at last seriously to method. Herman, Rivinus, and Ray severally proposed their own, but the immortal Tournefort carried away the prize from them all; he first ranged the whole vegetable kingdom systematically and, reforming the nomenclature in part, combined it by his new genera with that of Caspar Bauhin: but, far from freeing it of its long phrases, he either added new ones or loaded the old ones with additions, which his method obliged him to make. The barbarous custom was then introduced of tagging new names to the old ones by contradictory qui quae quod, making of the same plant two distinct genera.

For instance, "Dens Leonis qui Pilosella folio minus villoso. Doria quae Jacoboea orientalis limonii folio. Titanokeratophyton quod Lithophyton marinum albicans?"

Thus was the nomenclature loaded. The names of the plants became not only phrases but periods. I shall cite one of Plukenet's to prove that I do not exaggerate. "Gramen myloicophorum carolinianum seu gramen altissimum, panicula maxima speciosa, e spicis majoribus compressiusculis utrinque pinnatis blattam molendariam quodam modo referentibus, composita, foliis convolutis mucronatis pungentibus." Almag, 137.

It would have been all over with botany if this practice had continued; the nomenclature, now being absolutely insupportable, could no longer subsist in this state, and it was become necessary either that a reformation should be made or that the richest, the most lovely, and the easiest of the three parts of natural history should be abandoned.

At length, Linnaeus, full of his system and the vast ideas that it suggested to him, formed the project of newly molding the whole, a task that everybody felt the necessity of but no one dared to undertake. He did more; he executed it, and, having prepared in his *Critica Botanica* the rules by which it ought to be conducted, he determined the genera of plants in his *Genera Plantarum*, and afterward the species in his *Species Plantarum*, in such a manner that, by keeping all the old names that agreed with these new rules, and newly casting all the rest, he established at length a clear nomenclature, founded upon the true principles of the art that he had set forth. He preserved all the ancient genera that were truly natural; he corrected, simplified, united, or divided the rest as their true characters required. And in forming his names, he followed, sometimes even somewhat too severely, the rules that he had laid down.

# INTRODUCTION

With respect to the species, descriptions and distinctions were necessary to determine them; phrases therefore remained always indispensable, but, by confining himself to a small number of technical words, well chosen and well adapted, he made good short definitions deduced from the true character of the plant, banishing rigorously all that was foreign to it. For this it was necessary to create a new language for botany, which would spare the long periphrases of the old descriptions. Complaint has been made that the words of this language are not all to be found in Cicero. This complaint would be reasonable, had Cicero written a complete treatise of botany. Those words, however, are all either Greek or Latin, expressive, short, sonorous, and even form-elegant constructions by their extreme precision. It is in the constant practice of the art that we feel all the advantage of this new language, which is as convenient and necessary for botanists as that of algebra is to mathematicians.

Hitherto Linnaeus had indeed determined the greatest part of known plants, but he had not named them; for defining a thing is not naming it, a phrase can never be a true name, nor can it come into common use. He provided against this defect by the invention of trivial names, which he joined to the generic ones in order to distinguish the species. By this contrivance, the name of every plant is composed of only two words, which alone, when chosen with discernment and applied with propriety, often make the plant better known than the long phrases of Micheli and Plukenet. To be still better and more regularly acquainted with it, there is the phrase, which doubtless must be known but need not be repeated every time we have occasion to speak of the object.

Nothing is more pedantic or ridiculous when a woman, or one of those men who resemble women, is asking you the name of an herb or a flower in a garden, than to be under the necessity of answering by a long file of Latin words that have the appearance of magical incantation, an inconvenience sufficient to deter such frivolous persons from a charming study offered with so pedantic an apparatus.

However necessary or advantageous this reform might be, nothing less was wanting than Linnaeus's profound knowledge to execute it with success, and the reputation of this great naturalist to make it be universally adopted. It met with resistance at first and meets with it still. This could not be otherwise; his rivals in the same career look upon this adoption as a confession of inferiority that they do not like to make; his nomenclature seemed so much of a piece with his system that they could not well be separated. And botanists of the higher order, who think themselves obliged through pride not to adopt the system of any other, but each man to have his own, will not sacrifice their pretensions to the progress of an art for which the professors have rarely a disinterested fondness. National jealousies also oppose the admission of a foreign system. People think themselves obliged to support the famous men of their own country, especially after their death; for even that self-love, which made them scarcely bear their superiority while they were alive, is honored by their glory after they are departed. The great convenience, however, of this new nomenclature, and the utility of it, which practice has made known, have caused it to be adopted almost universally throughout Europe, sooner or later, and even in Paris, M. de Jussieu has established it in the royal garden, thus preferring the public utility to the glory of newly molding the whole, which the method of natural families invented by his illustrious uncle seemed to require.

Not that the nomenclature of Linnaeus is without its faults or gives no handle to criticism, but, until a more perfect one shall be found, in which nothing is wanting, it is far better to adopt this than to have none or to fall again into the phrases of Tournefort or Caspar Bauhin. I can even scarcely believe that a better nomenclature will in the future have success enough to proscribe this, to which the botanists of Europe are at present so wholly accustomed, and, having now the double tie of habit and convenience, they will renounce it with still more unwillingness than they found in adopting it. In order to bring about such a change, an author must be found with credit enough to efface that of Linnaeus, one to whose authority all Europe would be willing a second time to submit, which appears to me not likely to happen. For if his system, however excellent it may be, should be adopted by one nation only, it would throw botany into a new labyrinth and do it more injury than service.

Even the labor of Linnaeus, though immense, remains still imperfect, inasmuch as it does not comprehend all known plants and is not adopted by all botanists without exception, for the writings of such that do not submit to it require from their readers the same labor to settle the synonyms as they were forced to take for those that preceded it.

We are obliged to Mr. Crantz, notwithstanding his rage against Linnaeus, for having adopted his nomenclature, though he rejected his system. But Haller, in his large and excellent work on the Swiss plants, *Traité des plantes alpines*, rejects both, and Adanson does more, for he makes an entirely new nomenclature and furnishes no information whereby we may refer to it to Linnaeus's.

Haller always quotes the genus, and frequently specific characters of Linnaeus, but Adanson never quotes either. Haller attaches himself to an exact synonymy, by which, even when he does not add Linnaeus's enunciation of the species, we may find it at least indirectly by the relation of the synonyms. But Linnaeus and his books are absolutely null and void for M. Adanson and his readers, because the latter gives no information whereby we may connect them. So we are compelled to choose between Linnaeus and M. Adanson, who excludes him without mercy, and to throw all the works of one of them into the fire. Or else we must undertake a new work, which will be neither short nor easy, to connect these nomenclatures, which offer us no point of union.

Linnaeus indeed has not given a complete synonymy. For plants known long since, he has contented himself with quoting the Bauhins and Clusius, with a figure of each plant. For exotic plants lately discovered, he has cited one or two modern authors and the figures of Rheed, Rumphius, and some others and has gone no further. His undertaking did not require of him a more extended compilation, and it is sufficient that he has given one certain information with regard to every plant that he names.

Such is the present state of things. Now after this account of it, I would ask every reader of common sense, how it is possible to attach one's self to the study of plants, and at the same time to reject that of the nomenclature? It is just as if a man would make himself skillful in a language, with a determination not to learn the words of it. The names, it is true, are arbitrary; the knowledge of plants has no necessary connection with the nomenclature; and it is easy to conceive that an intelligent man might be an excellent botanist without knowing a single plant by its name.

# INTRODUCTION

But that one man alone, without books or any assistance from communicated information, should become of himself a very moderate botanist is a ridiculous assertion to make, and an enterprise impossible to execute. The question is whether three hundred years of study and observation should be lost to botany; whether three hundred volumes of figures and descriptions should be thrown into the fire; whether the knowledge acquired by all the learned, who have consecrated their purse, their life, their time, to distant, expensive, painful, and dangerous expeditions, should be useless to their successors; and whether everyone setting out from nothing could arrive by himself to the same knowledge that a long series of inquiry and study has spread over the mass of mankind? If not, and the third and most lovely part of natural history merits the attention of the curious, let them tell me how we shall manage to make use of the knowledge heretofore acquired, if we do not begin by learning the language of the writers and knowing to what objects the names employed by them belong. To admit therefore the study of botany, and to reject that of the nomenclature, is a most absurd contradiction.

| ATLAS OF ELEMENTARY BOTANY

# TABLE OF ILLUSTRATIONS

**LETTER** I · LILIACEOUS PLANTS

| | |
|---|---:|
| Asphodel | 15 |
| Hyacinth | 16 |
| Narcissus | 19 |
| Saffron | 21 |
| Tulip | 22 |

**LETTER** II · CRUCIFORM FLOWERS

| | |
|---|---:|
| Shepherd's purse | 27 |
| Scurvy grass | 28 |
| Wallflower | 31 |
| Dame's rocket | 33 |
| Penny grass | 34 |

**LETTER** III · PAPILIONACEOUS FLOWERS

| | |
|---|---:|
| Broom | 39 |
| Bean | 40 |
| Licorice | 43 |
| Sainfoin | 47 |

ATLAS OF ELEMENTARY BOTANY

**LETTER** IV · LABIATE FLOWERS

| | |
|---|---|
| Basilic | 50 |
| Cymbalaire | 53 |
| Lamier blanc | 55 |
| Pédiculaire | 56 |
| Sauge | 58 |

**LETTER** V · UMBELLATE PLANTS

| | |
|---|---|
| Cow parsnip | 63 |
| Field eryngo | 67 |
| Chervil | 68 |
| Cow weed | 71 |
| Parsley | 72 |

**LETTER** VI · COMPOUND FLOWERS

| | |
|---|---|
| Wormwood | 79 |
| Cornflower | 80 |
| Thistle | 83 |
| Daisy | 87 |
| Dandelion | 90 |

**LETTER** VII · FRUIT TREES

| | |
|---|---|
| Almond | 95 |
| Cherry | 97 |
| Plum | 98 |

**LETTER** VIII · HERBARIA

| | |
|---|---|
| Clover | 103 |

In the Same Collection

*Atlas of Dream Lands, Dominique Lanni, illustrations by Karin Doering-Froger, 2023*

*Atlas of Lost Civilizations, Dominique Lanni, illustrations by Camille Renversade 2025*

*Atlas of Extraterrestrial Zones, Bruno Fuligni, illustrations by François Moreno, 2023*

*Atlas of Lost Paradises, Gilles Lapouge, illustrations by Karin Doering-Froger, 2024*

*Atlas of Shipwrecks and Fortunes of the Sea, Cyril Hofstein, illustrations by Karin Doering-Froger, 2024*